GRAIN free
BRAIN food

CookNation

GRAIN free BRAIN food
LOSE THE GRAIN. CARE, FEED & SHARPEN YOUR BRAIN
OVER 80 DELICIOUS GLUTEN FREE RECIPES

ISBN 978-1-913174-03-3

DISCLAIMER

CONTENTS

INTRODUCTION

Foundations to a healthy diet with breakfast, lunch, dinner, dessert and snack recipes

Declining brain function is a major source of concern for us all. Symptoms of this decline may include difficulty with; memory loss, thinking speed, mental sharpness and quickness, language, understanding, judgment, mood, movement and carrying out daily activities.

The most devastating form of brain function decline is dementia (an umbrella term used to describe an ongoing decline in brain function). It is a damaging syndrome that is heartbreaking for families to deal with and many of us live with the fear of developing it. There are many different causes of dementia and there are different types. Vascular dementia (caused by restricted blood flow to the brain) and Alzheimer's disease (for which a cause is still unknown) are the two most common types.

According to the Alzheimer's Society, there are around 850,000 people in the UK suffering from dementia. One in 14 people over 65 will develop dementia, and a staggering 1 in 6 people over 80.

The way that our brain functions is still largely a mystery, an increasing number of studies suggest that the brain is sensitive to what we eat. Studies from respected medical sources have shown that a typical western diet, one that is high in grains and carbohydrates, can contribute to a number of serious medical conditions such as headaches, insomnia, epilepsy, anxiety, depression, attention deficit hyperactivity disorder (ADHD) and schizophrenia.

The link between diet and health has long been established and diets designed to reduce the risk of osteoporosis or heart disease are well established. Therefore, it surely makes sense that we can also use our food choices to prevent ourselves from developing brain disorders such as Alzheimer's.

Traditional medicines can be used to treat diseases and alleviate symptoms but, as the old adage goes, prevention is better than cure. Taking tablets is merely a way of tackling the symptoms, but not the underlying issue, which in Alzheimer's disease (as with a plethora of others) is thought to be inflammation.

By reducing inflammation in the brain, through removing harmful foods from our diet, we can reduce the instances of degenerative brain disorders. The most common foods which are harmful to our brains and cause inflammation are gluten (a protein found in wheat, barley and rye) and those that are high in carbohydrates.

By being able to identify the foods which have a negative impact on our health, we are able to remove them from our diets and embrace a new way of eating, securing our future brain health. In order to do this, you have to change your mindset away from the advice which we have been bombarded with over the last 50 years and embrace a diet that's as nature intended - free from high levels of carbohydrates, sugar and gluten.

The key messages that you need to absorb before embracing this way of life are:

SUGAR IS DANGEROUS
Research has concluded that elevated blood sugar levels are toxic to brain cells. Sugar can be found in lots of places you'd expect, such as cakes and chocolate, but is also prevalent in lots of processed food such as bread and pasta sauces. Carbohydrates metabolise into sugars, so eating a big bowl of white pasta does the same for your body as eating a Mars bar!

FAT IS GOOD
It may go against much of what you've been brought up to know about a healthy diet, but eating high levels of healthy fats will fuel your brain. It has also been shown in studies that those on a high fat-low carb diet actually have a lower level of bad cholesterol when compared to those who consume a low fat-high carb diet. Trans fats are still bad for you and you won't find them in these recipes, but high levels of olive oil, avocado, grass-fed beef, oily fish, nuts and seeds will keep you feeling full and your brain healthy, plus your food will taste delicious.

GLUTEN MUST GO
Gluten is a protein that has a debilitating affect on the brain. It causes sensitivities in many people and has been shown to cause inflammation throughout the body, as well as being linked to a number of serious illnesses. Although common, our bodies were not designed to eat wheat and therefore gluten. In order to ensure a healthy brain, it must be eliminated.

So now that you know the science and golden rules behind **GRAIN** free **BRAIN** food you must be wondering what you can and can't eat. The following lists should give you a good idea of what to eat using a traffic light system. **Red** foods should never be eaten, **amber** foods should be eaten in moderation (no more than one serving once a day) and **green** foods should be enjoyed in abundance.

GREEN FOODS

Eggs
Nut butters
Coconut oil
Extra-virgin olive oil
Ghee
Organic grass-fed butter
Avocados
Coconuts
Olives
Unsweetened nut milks
All roasted nuts except peanuts
(not salted or with any added
sugars)

All cheeses except blue or
processed (such as Dairylea)
Seeds
All herbs and spices
All vegetables apart from those
listed elsewhere
Low sugar fruits (such as berries
and citrus fruits)
Pickles
Fish
Shellfish
All grass-fed meats and organic
meat

AMBER FOODS

Buckwheat
Millet
Gluten free oats
Quinoa
Rice
Dried beans
Lentils
Carrots
Parsnips

Full fat dairy products
Sweet fruits (such as apples,
apricots or pineapple)
Natural sweeteners (such as stevia)
Dark chocolate (at least 70%
cacao)
Peanuts
Wine (preferably red)

RED FOODS

Bread and grains
Pasta
Sugar in any form (this includes
syrups)
Cereals
Crisps
Barley
Corn
Soy
Flour
Spelt
Trans fats (such as vegetable
shortening or margarine)
Couscous
Rye

Semolina
Cakes
Beer
Baked beans
Processed cooking oils (such as
canola)
Ketchup
Oats
Vodka
Any food labelled 'low-fat' unless
it's naturally so
Tofu
Dried fruits
Potatoes

So, now you have the building blocks to rid your food cupboards of any inflammation inducing grains and high-carbohydrate foods and stock it full of nourishing fats, proteins and vegetables. The next step is learning what to cook to ensure that keeping your brain healthy remains a delicious exercise. Ahead, you will find the foundations of a healthy diet with breakfast, lunch, dinner, dessert and snack recipes

• •

GRAIN free
BRAIN food

breakfast

BULLETPROOF COFFEE

Ingredients

- 1 cup hot coffee, freshly brewed
- 2 tbsp unsalted butter
- 1 tbsp MCT oil or coconut oil

Method

1 Combine all of the ingredients in a blender.

2 Blend until smooth and frothy. Then serve immediately.

CHEF'S NOTE

Although adding fat to coffee may seem like an odd choice, if you're someone who can't face a big meal first-thing then this is a great way of boosting your energy and cognitive performance levels.

STEAK AND EGGS

Ingredients

- 175g/6oz grass fed sirloin steak
- Olive or avocado oil spray
- 2 large eggs
- Pinch red pepper flakes

Method

1 Remove the steak from the fridge and season it with a pinch of salt and black pepper at least 10 mins before cooking.

2 Heat a griddle pan over a medium heat.

3 Spray the steak with oil. Griddle the steak, 2 minutes per side for medium-rare, or adjusted to suit your taste.

4 While the steak is cooking, heat a nonstick frying pan over medium heat.

5 When the steak is finished cooking, transfer it to a plate, loosely cover with foil and allow to rest.

6 While steak is resting, cook the eggs.

Spray the pan with oil. Break 2 eggs into it and fry them until whites are set.

7 Place the cooked eggs on a plate. Season them with a pinch of salt, pepper and the red pepper flakes before serving.

CHEF'S NOTE
Steak may seem like a decadent way to begin the day, but this dish is low carb, as well as high in protein and healthy fats, allowing you to feel fuller for longer.

BASIC OMELETTE

- 3 beaten eggs
- 1 tsp sunflower oil
- 1 tsp butter

Method

1 Season the beaten eggs well with salt and pepper.

2 Heat the oil and butter in a non-stick frying pan over a medium-low heat until the butter has melted and is foaming.

3 Pour the eggs into the pan, tilt the pan ever so slightly from one side to another to allow the eggs to swirl and cover the surface of the pan completely. Let the mixture cook for about 20 seconds, then scrape a line through the middle with a spatula.

4 Tilt the pan again to allow it to fill back up with the runny egg. Repeat once or twice more until the egg has just set.

5 Fold gently in half with the spatula. Slide onto a plate to serve.

CHEF'S NOTE
This omelette is adaptable to your tastes. Just before folding, fill with whatever you like. Try some grated cheese, sliced ham, fresh herbs, sautéed mushrooms or smoked salmon.

CHIA SEED PUDDING

Ingredients

- 175ml/6floz coconut milk
- 2 tbsp chia seeds
- ½ tsp vanilla extract

Method

1 Mix all of the ingredients in a non-metallic bowl or jar.

2 Cover, place in the fridge and leave overnight.

3 Serve the pudding with cream, coconut milk or some fresh or frozen berries.

CHEF'S NOTE
Naturally sweet, but with no added sugar, this is a great grab and go breakfast for those used to porridge or cereal in the morning.

SHAKSHUKA

Ingredients

- 1 tbsp olive oil
- 1 chopped large onion
- 1 red and 1 green pepper, cut into long slices
- 1 crushed clove of garlic
- ½ tsp cumin powder
- ½ tsp cayenne pepper
- 1 tbsp tomato purée
- 4 chopped salad tomatoes
- 4 eggs

To serve:
- 4 tbsp Greek yogurt

Method

1 Heat the olive oil in a large, lidded frying pan. Add the onions, peppers and garlic, then season with salt and pepper. Cook on a medium heat until soft. Add in the cumin and the cayenne pepper.

2 Stir in the tomato purée and cook for a couple more minutes before adding the tomatoes with a splash of water.

3 Simmer for 10 minutes or so, uncovered, until reduced a little and the tomatoes are soft. If it becomes too thick (it should have a pasta sauce consistency) then add a touch more water.

4 Make 4 small wells in the sauce and break an egg into each. Place the lid on the pan and cook for roughly 4 mins, or until the whites are just set and the yolks are still runny.

5 Serve with the yogurt drizzled on the top.

CHEF'S NOTE
This is a fantastic weekend brunch that feels special and easily scales up if your have friends or family staying.

BUCKWHEAT PANCAKES

Ingredients

- 2 eggs
- 250ml/8½floz milk
- 1 tsp vanilla extract
- 200g/7oz buckwheat flour
- 1½ tsp baking powder
- 1 tsp ground cinnamon
- Spray oil

Method

1 Whisk the eggs, milk and vanilla together in a jug.

2 Sieve the flour into a mixing bowl and add the baking powder and cinnamon. Gradually add the wet ingredients to the dry and whisk together. Add a pinch of salt and leave to rest for 1 hour.

3 Heat a spray of oil in a frying pan on a medium heat. Add a large spoonful of batter to the pan to make a pancake. Once golden, flip the pancake over. Repeat with the remaining batter until it's all used up. In between pancakes separate them with baking paper and keep warm in a low oven.

4 To serve put the pancakes on plates - top to your taste with fruit, yogurt, cream or shaved dark chocolate.

CHEF'S NOTE

Avoiding grains doesn't mean that pancakes have to be off the menu! Buckwheat is a distant relative of rhubarb and is naturally gluten free, with a delicate, nutty flavour.

BAKED AVOCADO

···················· Ingredients ····················

- · 2 medium sized avocados
- · 2 tbsp olive oil
- · 4 large eggs

···················· Method ····················

1 Preheat the oven to 190C/375F/ Gas 5 and line a baking sheet with tin foil.

2 Slice the avocados and remove the pits. Place the avocados on the baking sheet and use some scrunched-up foil to keep them in place, if necessary.

3 Scoop out a hole where the pit was and brush the avocado with olive oil.

4 Break an egg into the center of each of the avocados, being careful to keep the yolks intact. Season with salt and pepper.

5 Place in the oven and bake until the egg whites are completely set and

yolks begin to thicken, but are not hard - this should take around about 15 minutes. Serve.

CHEF'S NOTE
Avocados are full of healthy fats and take on a different, more nutty taste when served warm. Try them scattered with parsley, bacon bits, chopped chilli, seeds or spring onion for a different take.

CAULIFLOWER HASH BROWNS

Ingredients

- 450g/15oz cauliflower
- 3 eggs
- ½ grated white onion
- 1 tsp salt
- 2 pinches pepper
- 100g/4oz butter

Method

1 Peel away and discard the outer leaves and trim the cauliflower before grating using a food processor or grater.

2 Add the cauliflower to a large bowl. Add remaining ingredients and mix. Set aside for 5–10 minutes.

3 Melt a generous amount of butter or oil on medium heat in a large skillet.

4 Place the oven on a low heat to keep the first batches of hash browns warm while you make the others.

5 Place scoops of the grated cauliflower in the frying pan and flatten them carefully until they measure about 3-4 inches in diameter.

6 Fry for 4–5 mins on each side. Turn the heat down to make sure they don't burn.

7 Drain on a piece of kitchen towel if desired and serve.

CHEF'S NOTE

The perfect no-potato and no-grain accompaniment to breakfast. Hash browns go perfectly with bacon and eggs, or topped with sliced avocado and chilli.

CHAI LATTE

Ingredients

- 1 tbsp chai tea
- 475ml/15¾floz boiling water
- 75ml/2½floz double cream
- ½ tsp cinnamon
- ½ tsp ground ginger

Method

1 Brew the tea in the boiling water according to the packet instructions.

2 Leave to brew, be sure to let it get as much flavor as possible without it stewing.

3 Warm the cream with the spices in a small saucepan.

4 Add the cream to the tea and serve.

CHEF'S NOTE
A decadent and tasty beverage that feels like a meal in a glass due to the addition of double cream. A perfect alternative to sugar laden pumpkin spiced lattes.

BOILED EGGS WITH ASPARAGUS

Ingredients

- About 20 asparagus spears
- 2 large eggs
- 1 tbs unsalted butter
- A little cider vinegar

Method

1 Prepare the asparagus by snapping off any woody ends (the spears will break naturally where they are tender).

2 Simmer or steam the asparagus until tender but not too floppy - around 6mins.

3 Meanwhile, bring another pan of water to the boil. Carefully lower in the eggs and simmer for about 4 minutes.

4 Drain the asparagus well as soon as it is cooked and divide the spears between 2 warm plates. Transfer the eggs to egg cups and put them on the plates with the asparagus.

5 To eat, crack the egg and take off enough of the top to expose the runny yolk. Drop a piece of butter, a few drops of cider vinegar and some salt and pepper into the yolk, stir with a bit of asparagus, dip and eat. Add a little more butter, vinegar and seasoning as you go.

CHEF'S NOTE
This may seem an odd way of serving the boiled eggs, but the addition of the butter and vinegar gives you a short-cut, easy version of hollandaise sauce!

BLUEBERRY SMOOTHIE

·············· *Ingredients* ··················

- 200g/7oz coconut milk
- 125g/4oz frozen or fresh blueberries
- ½ tbsp lemon juice
- ¼ tsp vanilla extract

···················· *Method* ···················

1 Take the fruit from the freezer and leave to defrost for 10 mins.

2 Place all of the ingredients in a blender and mix until smooth.

3 Taste, and add more lemon juice if desired.

4 Serve immediately.

CHEF'S NOTE
Shop brought smoothies are convenient for busy days but are often full of sugar and bulked out with stabilisers that contain grains.

COCONUT PORRIDGE

•••••••••••••••••••• *Ingredients* ••••••••••••••••••••

- 50g/2oz butter or coconut oil
- 2 eggs
- 2 tbsp coconut flour
- 2 pinches ground psyllium husk powder

- 8 tbsp coconut cream
- 2 pinches salt

•••••••••••••••••••••••• *Method* ••••••••••••••••••••••••

1 Add all ingredients to a non-stick saucepan. Mix well and place over low heat. Stir constantly until you achieve your desired texture.

2 Serve with a swirl of double cream and topped with a few fresh or frozen berries, if desired.

CHEF'S NOTE
A warming breakfast for days when you require a comforting start. This version of porridge is less stodgy, keeping you feeling full but not sluggish.

SERVES 2

BANANA WAFFLES

Ingredients

- ¼ ripe banana
- 1 egg
- 3 tbsp almond flour
- 3 tbsp coconut milk
- ¼ tbsp ground psyllium husk powder

- A pinch of salt
- ¼ tsp baking powder
- A dash of vanilla extract
- ¼ tsp ground cinnamon

Method

1 Mix all of the ingredients together and let sit for half an hour.

2 Place the mix in a waffle maker and cook according to manufacturer's instructions.

3 Alternatively, fry the batter in melted butter in a pan over a medium heat, like pancakes.

4 Serve with hazelnut spread, cream or fresh berries.

CHEF'S NOTE
Psyllium husk powder is a form of fibre made from the seeds of the plantago plant. It acts in the same way as gluten in baking, gluing and holding ingredients together.

HUEVOS RANCHEROS

···· Ingredients ····

- 4 tbsp coconut oil
- 4 garlic cloves, minced
- 1 chopped orange pepper
- 1 chopped white onion
- 2 finely diced jalapeños
- 2 diced tomatoes
- 4 eggs
- 1 avocado
- 1 bunch of coriander

···· Method ····

1 Heat half of the coconut oil in a frying pan over medium heat.

2 Fry the garlic, pepper, onion and jalapeños for 3 minutes, or until the onion is translucent and the peppers have softened slightly.

3 Add the diced tomatoes and cook for 5 minutes, before setting aside.

4 Place a separate nonstick pan over medium-low heat and add the remaining coconut oil.

5 Slow-cook the eggs for approximately 6 mins or until the whites cook through.

6 Plate the eggs, top with the vegetable mix, and garnish with coriander and avocado slices.

CHEF'S NOTE
A spicy and zingy start to the day, these eggs can be served with chilli sauce if you like heat, or tamed with some sour cream.

GRAIN-FREE GRANOLA

Ingredients

- 225g/8oz unsweetened coconut flakes
- 2 medium ripe bananas
- 1 grated apple
- 2 tbsp melted coconut oil
- 1½ tsp cinnamon
- 1 tsp ground ginger
- ½ tsp ground mace
- ¼ tsp sea salt

Method

1 Preheat your oven to 150C/300F/ Gas 2 and line a baking sheet with parchment paper.

2 Mash the banana until smooth, then stir in the coconut oil, grated apple, spices, and sea salt.

3 Add the wet ingredients to the dry mixture and stir until well combined and everything sticks together.

4 Spread out evenly onto the prepared baking sheet.

5 Bake for 45 to 50 mins, stirring halfway through, until the granola is a golden brown.

6 Leave to cool for at least 15 mins to set. Break any large chunks into smaller, bite-sized pieces.

CHEF'S NOTE
Granola is great to batch cook and have on the go for breakfast served with full fat yogurt or milk. This version contains some amber food so it is best to only have it occasionally.

GREEK YOGHURT WITH RASPBERRIES AND ALMONDS

Ingredients

- 250ml/8½floz full fat Greek yoghurt
- 1 handful fresh raspberries
- 1 handful dry roasted almonds

Method

1 Place the yoghurt in a bowl.

2 Roughly chop the almonds.

3 Stir the yoghurt through with most of the nuts and berries.

4 Scatter the remaining nuts and berries on the top and serve.

CHEF'S NOTE
Ludicrously simple, this is more of a blueprint than a recipe. Try with strawberries and pecans or blueberries and cashews.

OATY BREAKFAST BOWL

Ingredients

- 50g/2oz jumbo gluten free porridge oats
- 200ml/7floz unsweetened almond milk
- ½ tsp vanilla extract
- 2 tbsp natural yogurt
- 25g/1oz chia seeds

Method

1 Mix all of the ingredients in a bowl and leave to soak for at least 20 mins until the oats have softened.

2 If the porridge is too dry after this time, add a little water.

3 Divide the mixture between 2 bowls and top each with blueberries, flaked almonds and honey, or any other combination of fruit and nuts you would prefer.

CHEF'S NOTE

This breakfast bowl is good to make the night before a busy morning. Make sure your oats are gluten free so this can be a delicious, occasional treat.

GRAIN free
BRAIN food

lunches

TURKEY TONNATO

Ingredients

- 100g/3½oz mayonnaise
- 1 tbsp capers
- 2 tinned anchovies
- 80g/3oz tuna in oil, drained
- Juice ½ lemon
- 400g/14oz roast turkey
- 100g/3½oz bag rocket

Method

1 Put the mayonnaise, most of the capers, 1 whole anchovy, the tuna and most of the lemon juice into a food processor.

2 Blitz until the tuna is completely mixed into the mayonnaise. Season with pepper, taste, and add salt and more lemon juice, if needed. If your sauce seems a bit thick, mix in a drop of water.

3 Divide the turkey and rocket over 4 plates, then spoon over the dressing and scatter with the remaining capers and sliced anchovy before serving.

CHEF'S NOTE
An unusual and delicious lunch, this transports well if the dressing is kept separately and poured over just before serving. Perfect for post-Christmas leftovers.

CHICKEN CAESAR SALAD

Ingredients

For the Salad:
- 4 slices of prosciutto
- 2 cornfed chicken breasts, bone and skin removed
- 2 cos lettuces

For the dressing:
- 2 garlic cloves

- 75ml/3floz white wine
- 2 eggs, yolks only
- 1 anchovy fillet
- 75g/3oz Parmesan cheese, grated
- 150ml/5floz extra virgin olive oil
- 2 tsp Dijon mustard

Method

1 Preheat your grill to a high heat.

2 Place the prosciutto onto a baking sheet and place under the grill for 3-4 mins, or until crisp. Remove and place on a plate lined with kitchen paper to drain.

3 Cut both chicken breasts through the middle, without cutting through, to form one large flat piece. Season, to taste, with salt and black pepper and brush with olive oil.

4 Heat a griddle pan until hot, then place the chicken breasts on it and cook for 2-3 mins on each side, or until just cooked through.

5 Separate the leaves from the lettuce and cut into chunky pieces.

6 For the dressing, in a medium saucepan, bring the garlic and wine to a boil and simmer for about 5 mins, until the garlic has softened. Leave to cool.

7 Combine the wine and garlic with the egg yolks, anchovy and cheese in a mixing bowl. Blend with a hand blender or food processor until smooth. Drizzle in the oil in a thin, steady stream, taking care not to add it too quickly, otherwise it could split and curdle. Stir in the mustard and add seasoning to taste.

8 Add the crispy prosciutto and lettuce to the dressing and toss to combine.

9 To serve, place the salad on a plate, top with the chicken and pour the dressing over.

CREAM OF TOMATO SOUP

Ingredients

- 3 tbsp olive oil
- 1 large chopped onion
- 2 crushed garlic cloves
- 2 chopped celery sticks
- 200g/7oz chopped carrots
- 1 bay leaf
- 1 large sprig fresh thyme
- 750g/1½lb roughly chopped ripe plum or vine-ripened tomatoes
- 200ml/7floz passata
- 500ml/17floz vegetable stock
- 100ml/3½floz single cream
- A splash of dry sherry

Method

1 Heat the olive oil in a large saucepan and cook the onion for 5-6 mins over a gentle heat until almost softened, but not browned. Add the garlic, celery, carrots, bay leaf and thyme and cook for a further 6-7 mins, stirring occasionally to make sure the vegetables don't stick to the bottom of the pan.

2 Add the chopped tomatoes and season well with salt and pepper. Cook for a few minutes, then stir in the passata and vegetable stock. Bring to a simmer, cover with a lid and cook for 35-40 minutes, until all of the vegetables are tender.

3 Remove the bay leaf and thyme, then blend the soup in a liquidizer or food processor. Pour the soup into a clean saucepan, passing it through a sieve if you want it really smooth. Stir in the cream, a splash of sherry and extra seasoning, if required.

4 Pour into large mugs or bowls and serve.

CHEF'S NOTE
Tinned or pre-prepared soups are often full of sugar. Make your own to ensure all-natural ingredients. If using a stock cube, check that it's gluten free.

GREEK SALAD

Ingredients

- ½ small red onion, thinly sliced
- 2 large roughly chopped, ripe tomatoes
- ½ cucumber, deseeded and roughly chopped
- 100g/3½oz feta cheese
- 50g/1¾oz black olives, pitted

  and drained
- Small handful fresh mint leaves
- ½ tsp dried oregano
- 2 tsp extra virgin olive oil
- 2 tsp fresh lemon juice

Method

1 Cube the feta cheese.

2 Put the onion, tomatoes and cucumber in a bowl and season to taste.

3 Scatter the feta, olives and mint leaves on top.

4 Sprinkle over the oregano and toss lightly. Drizzle over the oil and lemon juice, then serve.

CHEF'S NOTE

Greek salad is fresh, zingy and full of healthy fats. A lovely lunch on its own, or try served with leftover roast chicken.

SPANISH-STYLE OMELETTE

Ingredients

- 6 eggs
- 2 tbs butter
- 4 stalks celery chopped into small slices
- 175g/6oz baby spinach
- 2 tsp turmeric
- 2 tsps cumin

Method

1 Melt the butter in a heated frying pan. Fry the celery slices with the spices, salt and pepper for 3-5 mins over a medium-low heat or until soft.

2 Add the spinach and mix well.

3 Beat the eggs in a jug.

4 Move the vegetable mix to the side of the pan and pour in the beaten eggs on the other side of the pan.

5 Gently fold the vegetable mix onto the eggs and cook for 2-3 minutes.

CHEF'S NOTE
This omelette tastes good hot or cold, so makes a great lunch to make ahead of time to take to work or for a picnic.

COBB SALAD

Ingredients

For the salad:
- 2 eggs
- 75g/3oz bacon
- ½ roast chicken
- 50g/2oz blue cheese
- 1 avocado
- 1 tomato
- 150g/5oz iceberg lettuce
- 1 tbsp fresh chives (optional)
- salt and ground black pepper

For the dressing:
- 3 tbsp mayonnaise
- 1 tbsp ranch seasoning
- 2 tbsp water

Method

1 Start by making the dressing. Combine the mayonnaise, ranch seasoning and water. Season with salt and pepper, and set aside.

2 Place the eggs in boiling water for 8-10 mins. Cool and then peel and roughly chop.

3 Fry the bacon in a hot dry pan until crispy. Cut the chicken into small pieces and chop up the vegetables to roughly the same size. Crumble in the blue cheese.

4 Distribute everything on a bed of shredded lettuce. Season with salt and pepper and drizzle with the dressing, then top with finely chopped chives.

CHEF'S NOTE
This salad is anything but bland - it is packed full of strong flavours from the blue cheese, bacon and chicken. A perfect lunch that can be made in advance of serving.

CHICKEN KEBABS

Ingredients

- 3 tbsp natural yoghurt
- 1 tsp garam masala or curry powder
- 1 tsp chilli powder
- 2 tsp lime or lemon juice

- 2 tsp fresh chopped coriander, (optional)
- 1 fresh red chilli, finely chopped
- 4 x 150g/5oz chicken breasts, cubed

Method

1 Mix together the yoghurt, garam masala, chilli powder, lime juice, coriander and red chilli.

2 Marinate the chicken in the yoghurt mixture for 5 minutes.

3 Preheat a griddle pan to hot.

4 Thread the chicken onto kebab skewers and cook on the griddle until it is tender and cooked all the way through.

CHEF'S NOTE
These kebabs are delicious served hot or cold. Have with salad or, alternatively, try making lettuce wraps with yoghurt and chilli sauce.

DORO WAT SOUP

Ingredients

- 2 tbps coconut oil
- ½ medium onion, finely chopped
- 1 garlic clove, minced
- ½ tbsp berbere seasoning
- 1 tsp fine sea salt

- 325g/12oz boneless, skinless chicken breasts, cut into ¾-inch chunks
- 475ml/15¾floz chicken stock
- 4 hard-boiled eggs

Method

1 Heat the oil in a large saucepan. Once melted, add the onion, garlic, berbere seasoning and salt. Then cook for 10 mins or until the onion starts to caramelise.

2 Add the chicken and stock, place a lid on the pan and cook for an hour.

3 Slice each hard-boiled egg in half. Serve the soup in bowls with half an egg.

CHEF'S NOTE

Berbere is an unusual and delicious spice mix that is widely used in Ethiopia and Eritrea. It is made of chilli peppers, garlic, ginger, basil, korarima, rue, ajwain, nigella, and fenugreek.

GRAIN FREE WRAPS

Ingredients

- 2 eggs
- 2 egg whites
- 150g/5oz cream cheese
- 1½ tsp ground psyllium husk powder
- 1 tbsp coconut flour
- ½ tsp salt

Method

1 Preheat the oven to 200C/400F/ Gas 6.

2 Beat the eggs and egg whites until fluffy. Add the cream cheese and mix until the batter is smooth.

3 Mix together the salt, psyllium husk and coconut flour in a small bowl. Add the flour mixture to the batter, one spoonful at a time, and mix well. Let the batter sit for a few minutes, until it gets thick, like pancake batter.

4 Bring out two baking sheets and place parchment paper on each. Using a spatula, spread the batter thinly (no more than ¼ inch thick) in 4–6 circles.

5 Bake on upper rack for about 5 mins or until the tortilla turns a little brown around the edges. Carefully check the bottom side so that it doesn't burn.

CHEF'S NOTE
Shop brought wraps may be out of bounds if you wish to keep a healthy brain, but this grain-free version is just as tasty wrapped around your favourite fillings.

FRENCH ONION SOUP

Ingredients

- 50g/2oz butter
- 1kg/2lb4oz onions, thinly sliced
- 2 garlic cloves, chopped
- 100ml/3½floz white wine
- 2 tbsp Madeira, plus extra once

- cooked, to taste
- 1ltr/1¾pt fresh beef stock
- Salt and freshly ground black pepper

Method

1 Melt the butter in a medium-sized pan, add the onions and garlic and gently fry over a low heat for 30-35 minutes, stirring occasionally, until the onions are really soft.

2 Add the white wine, stirring the bottom of the pan to loosen the browned onion. Bring it back to the boil then add the Madeira and beef stock.

3 Bring to the boil and then lower the heat and simmer for about 10-12 mins.

4 Taste the soup to check the

seasoning, and add salt and freshly ground black pepper to taste. Add another few tablespoons of Madeira to the soup, to boost the flavour, and stir well.

CHEF'S NOTE

Many soups contain flour to thicken, but by taking your time to properly caramelise the onions, you'll have a perfect rich and sticky base that makes it unnecessary.

39

BAKED EGGS

Ingredients

- 1 tbsp butter
- 2 spring onions, chopped
- 60g/2oz chopped ham
- 4 tbsp double cream
- 4 eggs

Method

1 Preheat the oven to 160C/325F/Gas 3. Heat the butter in a small pan and fry the spring onions until crispy. Add the ham and cook for another minute. Remove and drain on a paper towel.

2 Divide the ham and spring onions between four ramekins, then pour in the cream and season well. Break an egg into each ramekin.

3 Place the ramekins in a deep roasting tin, then pour in boiling water until it reaches half-way up the side of each ramekin. Bake for 10-12 mins, or until firm.

4 Serve immediately with a dressed green salad.

CHEF'S NOTE

Baked eggs take on an extra rich and luxurious texture that makes them perfect for an indulgent lunch or light supper.

SCALLOPS AND CHORIZO

Ingredients

- 3 fresh chorizo sausages, sliced into rounds the width of a pound coin
- 4 spring onions, trimmed and sliced
- 2 red chillies, thickly sliced
- 24 scallops, cleaned (with 6 shells reserved and cleaned if you can get them)
- Juice of 1 lemon

Method

1 Heat a heavy griddle pan over a high heat.

2 Fry the chorizo until it is browned and some of the juices are running into the pan.

3 Add the spring onion and chilli and fry for 2-3 mins.

4 Add the scallops and fry for 2-3 mins on either side, or until cooked through. Squeeze over the lemon juice and stir to coat.

5 Divide the scallops and chorizo among the six scallop shells and serve.

CHEF'S NOTE
A perfect balance of sweet and savory- the sweet scallop meat combines wonderfully with the spicy depth of the chorizo for a delicious light meal.

VEGGIE BAKE

······················· *Ingredients* ·····················

- 2 large field mushrooms
- 4 halved tomatoes
- 1 thinly sliced garlic clove

- 2 tsp olive oil
- 200g/7oz spinach
- 2 eggs

························· *Method* ·························

1 Preheat the oven to 200C/180C fan/gas 6. Put the mushrooms and tomatoes into an ovenproof dish. Scatter over the garlic and drizzle over the oil with some seasoning, before baking for 10 mins.

2 Whilst it's cooking, put the spinach into a large colander, then pour over a kettle of boiling water to wilt it. Squeeze out any excess water before adding to the dish.

3 Make 2 little gaps between the vegetables and crack the eggs into them. Return to the oven and cook for a further 8-10 mins or until the egg is cooked to your liking.

CHEF'S NOTE
This veggie bake contains three of your five a day and makes a great light meal. Serve with chilli sauce if you like more kick.

GARLIC MUSHROOM FRITTATA

Ingredients

- 1 tbsp olive oil
- 250g/9oz sliced chestnut mushrooms
- 1 crushed garlic clove
- 1 tbsp thinly sliced fresh chives
- 4 large beaten eggs
- freshly ground black pepper

Method

1 Heat the oil in a small frying pan over a high heat. Stir-fry the mushrooms in three batches for 2-3 mins, or until softened. Tip the cooked mushrooms into a sieve and drain the excess cooking juice.

2 Return all the mushrooms to the pan and stir in the garlic and chives with a pinch of ground black pepper. Cook for a further minute, then reduce the heat to low.

3 Preheat the grill to its hottest setting. Pour the eggs over the mushrooms. Cook for five mins, or until almost set.

4 Place the pan under the grill for 3-4 mins until set. Serve immediately, or allow to cool.

CHEF'S NOTE
Mushrooms and eggs are high in protein and make a quick, filling meal at any time of the day. This frittata makes a great lunch or light dinner, served with salad.

AVOCADO CHICKEN SALAD

Ingredients

- 1 cooked chicken breast
- 1 ripe avocado pitted and diced
- 1 small chopped red or green pepper
- 1 tbsp chopped coriander
- 1 tbsp lime juice
- 1 tbsp olive oil

Method

1 In a large bowl, add the shredded chicken, avocado, onion, pepper and coriander.

2 Squeeze over the lime juice, olive oil, then season with salt and pepper. Toss gently until all the Ingredients are combined and serve.

CHEF'S NOTE
Avocados are full of healthy fats that will help keep you feeling full and healthy. This salad works well with leftover roast chicken, or try adding bacon bits.

VIETNAMESE CHICKEN SALAD

Ingredients

- 1 head Chinese leaf or ½ iceberg lettuce, shredded
- 2 cooked chicken breasts, shredded
- 1 mango, peeled, stoned and thinly sliced
- 10 fresh mint leaves

- 6 spring onions, sliced diagonally
- 3 tbsp salted peanuts, roughly chopped
- For the dressing:
- Juice 4 limes
- 4 tbsp sesame oil
- A splash of fish sauce

- 2 large red chillies, deseeded and finely chopped

Method

1 First, make the dressing by mixing together all the ingredients.

2 Then, in a large bowl, mix all the salad ingredients, except the nuts.

3 Toss with the dressing and season with black pepper.

4 Scatter the nuts on top to serve.

CHEF'S NOTE
The balance of sweet, spicy, hot and sour flavours and soft, crisp and crunchy textures make this an addictive salad. Make sure your fish sauce is gluten free and only have occasionally, due to the sugary mango.

TANGY TUNA LETTUCE WRAPS

Ingredients

- 2 drops rapeseed oil
- 2 x 140g/4½oz tuna fillets
- 1 ripe avocado
- ½ tsp English mustard powder
- 1 tsp cider vinegar
- 1 tbsp capers
- 8 romaine lettuce leaves
- 16 halved cherry tomatoes

Method

1 Brush the tuna with a little oil. Heat a non-stick pan, add the tuna and cook for 1 min each side, or a min or so longer for a thicker fillet. Transfer to a plate to rest.

2 Halve and stone the avocado and scoop the flesh into a small bowl.

3 Add the mustard powder and vinegar, then mash well so that the mixture is smooth, like mayonnaise.

4 Stir in the capers. Spoon into two small dishes and put on serving plates with the lettuce leaves, and tomatoes.

5 Slice the tuna (it should be slightly pink inside).

6 Spoon some 'mayo' on the lettuce leaves and top with tuna and cherry tomatoes and a few extra capers. To eat, roll up into little wraps.

CHEF'S NOTE
Replacing your usual slices of bread with lettuce is a great way to enjoy your usual sandwich or wrap fillings in a grain-free way.

GRAIN free
BRAIN food

main meals

TROUT WRAPPED IN BACON

·················· *Ingredients* ··················

- 4 trout fillets
- 4 strips thick cut bacon
- Juice of 1 lemon

- 2 sprigs thyme
- Green salad to serve

·················· *Method* ··················

1 Season the fish and sprinkle with thyme leaves, then squeeze the lemon over the fillets.

2 Wrap each fillet in the bacon and fry in a hot pan for around 3 mins a side or until the bacon is crispy.

3 Serve immediately with a crisp green salad.

CHEF'S NOTE
Trout is a delicious oily fish that's strong enough to withstand the taste of the bacon. Pour the pan juices over the salad leaves for a dressing that's out of this world!

VENISON STEW

Ingredients

- 12 shallots
- 2 tbsp olive oil, plus extra for brushing
- 1 sprig of fresh thyme
- 1kg/2¼lb boned venison loin

- 2 tbsp grated fresh horseradish
- 200ml/7floz crème fraîche
- 1 tsp white wine vinegar
- 1 sprig of fresh rosemary
- Zest of 1 orange

Method

1 Preheat the oven to 180°C/350°F/Gas 4. Toss the unpeeled shallots in the olive oil, season with sea salt and black pepper, then place them in a shallow baking dish with the thyme sprig. Cover tightly with foil and bake in the oven for 45mins or until soft.

2 Meanwhile, preheat a heavy griddle pan large enough to hold the venison comfortably. Remove all the fat and any sinew from the venison, season well and brush with olive oil. Place on the hot griddle to sear and brown all over – about 2-3mins. Take out of the pan and place on a plate to cool.

3 Mix the horseradish into the crème fraîche. Season it well with salt, pepper and vinegar.

4 Finely chop the rosemary and finely grate the zest of the orange.

5 Thinly slice the venison with a sharp carving knife and lay 3 slices on each plate. Peel some of the warm shallots, tear them in half and lay a piece on top of each piece of venison. Spoon a little horseradish crème fraîche on top and sprinkle the plates with the rosemary and orange zest before serving.

CHEF'S NOTE
Venison is served rarely enough to make it feel like a real treat. Try serving with buttery mashed celeriac.

PORK RAGÙ

····· Ingredients ·····

- 700g/1lb9oz boneless pork shoulder
- 5tbsp vegetable oil
- 4 rashers smoked streaky bacon or pancetta, cut into 1cm slices
- 1 large onion, finely chopped
- 4 garlic cloves, crushed
- 75g/3oz pitted black olives

- 500ml/2 cups red wine
- 400g/14oz tinned chopped tomatoes
- 2tbsp tomato puree
- 500ml beef stock
- 2 large bay leaves
- 3 sprigs thyme
- 1 rosemary stalk, chopped

····· Method ·····

1 Cut the pork into chunky pieces, each about 2.5cm. Trim off any really hard or excessive fat as you go. Season the meat well with salt and pepper.

2 Heat 2 tablespoons of oil in a large frying pan.

3 Fry the chunks of pork over a medium-high heat until browned on all sides, turning every now and then. This may take a few batches. As the meat browns, transfer it to a large flameproof casserole dish.

4 Add a little more oil to the pan in which you browned the pork and fry the bacon for 2–3 minutes, until brown and crispy, then scatter it over the meat.

5 In the same pan, fry the onion over a low heat for 5 mins. Stir in the garlic and olives and cook for 2 mins, Add to the meat and pour in the wine. Stir in the tomatoes, tomato puree and beef stock. Add all the herbs and bring to a simmer.

6 Stir well and cover with a lid. Turn the heat down low and gently simmer for 2½ hours, or until the meat is completely tender.

7 Remove the lid every now and then and stir. If the liquid reduces too much, add a little extra water. The sauce should be fairly thick at the end of the cooking time. Remove the thyme and rosemary stalks and bay leaves, then season to taste.

8 Serve with freshly grated Parmesan.

PERFECT ROAST CHICKEN

········ *Ingredients* ········

- · 1 large chicken
- · 1 lemon

- · 2 tbsp butter
- · Flaky sea salt

········ *Method* ········

1 Preheat the oven to 220C/425F/Gas 7.

2 Cut the lemon in half and scatter a little salt over the cut side before placing inside the chicken cavity

3 Spread the butter over the chicken skin and then place it in the oven for 1 hour, or until the skin is crispy and the juices run clear when a skewer is inserted into the fattest part.

4 Remove the chicken from the oven, squeeze the juice from the remaining lemon half over the chicken and sprinkle some salt over.

CHEF'S NOTE
A roast chicken has to be one of the most inviting scents in the world. Worth making, even if there's only 1 or 2 of you, as leftover chicken will always be welcome.

LAMB STEW

Ingredients

- 750g/1lb10oz lamb neck fillet, cut into 2.5cm/1in cubes
- Salt and freshly ground black pepper
- 1tbsp olive oil
- 50g/2oz butter
- 12 baby onions, peeled
- 2 medium carrots, diced
- 1 medium swede, diced
- 50ml/2floz white wine
- 2 sprigs rosemary
- 4 bay leaves
- 1¼l/1.6pt lamb stock
- 3 tbsp flat leaf parsley, roughly chopped

Method

1 Preheat the oven to 120C/250F/Gas ½.

2 Season the lamb. Place a heavy-bottom casserole dish over a medium heat, add the olive oil and butter, then the lamb. Fry until golden brown. Remove the lamb and keep to one side.

3 Reduce the heat and fry the onions, carrots and swede until caramelised. Add the wine and simmer until the liquid has reduced by half, then add the lamb back in, along with the lamb stock. Bring the stew to a simmer, then add the bay leaf and rosemary. Cover with a lid, transfer the pan to the oven and bake for 1 hour.

4 Add the parsley to the casserole dish and serve equally between four shallow bowls.

CHEF'S NOTE
Lamb may have gone out of fashion for a time as people desired low fat meats, but now we know better we should enjoy the delicious flavour that it provides.

STEAK WITH BEARNAISE SAUCE

Ingredients

- 4 steaks of your choice, cooked to your taste
- 300g/10½oz butter
- 4tbsp white wine vinegar
- 4 shallots, chopped
- 3 tbsp chopped fresh tarragon, plus 2 tbsp whole tarragon leaves
- 4 free-range egg yolks
- 1 tsp lemon juice

Method

1 Melt the butter in a small, heavy-based saucepan over a low heat. When the butter is foaming, remove the pan from the heat and leave it to stand for a few minutes so that the white solids sink to the bottom of the pan. Sieve the butter through a fine sieve and discard the solids.

2 Pour the vinegar into a small pan. Add the shallots, chopped tarragon and salt, to taste. Heat gently over a medium heat until the liquid has reduced by more than half. Strain and set aside until completely cool

3 Lightly beat the egg yolks with a teaspoon of water. Stir the egg yolk mixture into the cooled vinegar, then add the lemon juice.

4 Pour the mixture into a bowl suspended over a pan of simmering water (do not allow base of the bowl to touch the water). Whisk constantly until the sauce has thickened enough to coat the back of a spoon and has increased in volume.

5 Remove the bowl from the heat and slowly pour in the butter in a steady stream, whisking continuously, until the mixture is thick and smooth. Fold in the tarragon leaves and season, to taste, with salt and freshly ground black pepper.

6 Serve the sauce poured over the steaks.

RABBIT CASSEROLE

Ingredients

- 2 rabbits, jointed
- 6 tbsp olive oil
- 4 garlic cloves, crushed
- 1 sprig fresh rosemary
- 2 bay leaves
- 568ml/16floz dry white wine
- ½ lemon, juice only
- 55g/2oz almond flour
- 1 sliced onion
- 1 sliced celery stalk
- 8 anchovy fillets in oil
- 85g/3oz capers

Method

1 Place the rabbit pieces into a large bowl and add three tablespoons of the olive oil, the garlic, rosemary, bay leaves, white wine and lemon juice. Stir until well combined, then cover and marinate in the fridge overnight.

2 Preheat the oven to 170C/325F/Gas 3.

3 Remove the rabbit pieces from the marinade (but keep the marinade) and pat dry with kitchen paper. Dust the rabbit pieces in the flour and shake off any excess.

4 Heat the remaining olive oil in a large pan over a medium heat. Add the rabbit pieces to the hot oil and fry for 4-5 minutes or until golden brown all over. Transfer to an ovenproof casserole dish.

5 Pour the reserved marinade into the hot frying pan and warm through, then pour it into the casserole with the rabbit. Add the onion and celery to the casserole and cook in the oven for 45 minutes, or until the rabbit is tender. Add the anchovies and capers and cook for another 15 minutes.

CHEF'S NOTE
Rabbit is a tasty meat that's strong enough to take the rich flavours in this casserole. Freeze any leftovers for a delicious and easy meal another day.

ROAST LAMB

············ *Ingredients* ··················

- 1 leg of lamb
- 1 tsp of chopped rosemary
- 1 tbsp olive oil
- 2 crushed cloves of garlic

···················· *Method* ··················

1 Rub all of the ingredients over the lamb and leave to marinate for at least an hour or preferably overnight.

2 Preheat the oven to 220C/425F/Gas 7.

3 Cook the lamb in a roasting tin for around 1hr 15mins. The outside should be crispy and the meat slightly pink inside.

CHEF'S NOTE
A roast dinner is a feast fit for a king. This lamb goes wonderfully with roasted root vegetables and homemade mint sauce.

SERVES 2

PESTO CHICKEN BAKE

······· *Ingredients* ·······

- · 2 chicken breasts
- · 2 slices prosciutto
- · 100g/3½oz crème fraîche
- · 1½ tbsp pesto
- · 25g grated Parmesan
- · 1 tbsp pine nuts

······ *Method* ······

1 Heat oven to 200C/180C fan/Gas 6.

2 Season the chicken all over, then wrap each fillet in a slice of ham. Put into a large baking dish.

3 Dot the crème fraîche between the breasts and over the exposed ends of the chicken. Dot the pesto around the chicken. Scatter the cheese over the top.

4 Bake the chicken for 25-30 mins, adding the pine nuts halfway through, until the crème fraîche has made a sauce around the chicken, and the cheese and ham are turning golden.

CHEF'S NOTE

Full of healthy fats, this delicious dish goes well when served with streamed green vegetables or mashed cauliflower-perfect for soaking up the tasty sauce.

56

ZESTY FISH STEW

Ingredients

- Handful flat-leaf parsley leaves, chopped
- 1 garlic clove, finely chopped
- Zest and juice 1 lemon
- 2 tbsp olive oil
- 1 small onion, finely sliced
- 1 tsp paprika
- Pinch cayenne pepper
- 400g/14oz tined chopped tomatoes
- 1 fish stock cube
- 100g/3½oz raw peeled king prawns
- 410g/14oz dried, soaked chickpeas
- 250g/9oz skinless fish fillets, cut into large chunks

Method

1 In a small bowl, mix the parsley with ½ the garlic and lemon zest, then set aside. Heat 2 tbsp oil in a large sauté pan. Add the onion and sweat for about 5 mins until the onion has softened. Add the remaining oil, garlic and spices, then cook for 2 mins more.

2 Pour over the lemon juice and sizzle for a moment. Add the tomatoes and crumble in the stock. Season with a little salt, then cover the pan. Simmer everything for 15-20 mins.

3 Stir through the prawns and chickpeas and nestle the fish chunks into the top of the stew.

4 Reduce the heat and re- cover the pan, then cook for about 8 mins, stirring very gently once or twice. When the fish is just cooked through, remove from the heat, scatter with the parsley mix to serve.

CHEF'S NOTE
This recipe is easy to scale up or can be adapted to use chicken instead of fish. The chickpeas make this an amber food that's perfect to serve to guests.

SERVES 4

VEGETABLE CURRY

Ingredients

- 1 tbsp ghee
- 2 onions, finely chopped
- 250g/9oz mixed chopped veg
- 2 garlic cloves, crushed
- 20g/¾oz ginger, finely grated
- 2 tsp garam masala
- ½ tsp hot chilli powder
- 400g/14oz tinned chopped tomatoes
- 600ml/20fl oz chicken stock
- 100g/3½oz red split lentils
- 2 bay leaves
- 200g/7oz brown rice
- To serve: 150g/5oz yoghurt
- 1 tbsp chopped coriander

Method

1 Place the ghee in a large saucepan over a medium heat. Cook the onions for 5 minutes, stirring regularly, until softened and very lightly browned.

2 Stir in the garlic, ginger, garam masala and chilli powder and cook for a few seconds, stirring constantly.

3 Tip the tomatoes into the pan and add the chicken stock, lentils and bay leaves. Bring to the boil, cover loosely with a lid and simmer gently for 35 minutes, or until the vegetables are tender and the lentils have completely broken down, stirring occasionally. Remove the lid for the last 10 mins of cooking time, stirring so the lentils don't stick.

4 About 25 minutes before the curry is ready, cook the rice in plenty of boiling water until tender, then drain well.

5 Season the curry to taste. Serve with the rice, topped with yoghurt and sprinkled with coriander.

CHEF'S NOTE
Takeaways can be difficult when you're regulating your diet as it's hard to always know what is in it. Make your own for a tastier and healthier take.

58

AUBERGINE BAKE

Ingredients

- 6 large beef tomatoes-tops sliced off a quarter of the way down the tomato and reserved, seeds and pulp scooped out and reserved
- 9 tbsp extra virgin olive oil,
- 1 small onion, chopped

- 2 handfuls fresh basil leaves
- 2-3 tbsp gluten-free flour
- 400g/14oz small aubergines, thinly sliced into rounds
- 2 free-range eggs, beaten with a large pinch of salt
- 200g/7oz smoked mozzarella

Method

1 Preheat the oven to 200C/400F/Gas 6. Add a pinch of salt to the cavity of each tomato. Turn upside down and set aside for 10 minutes.

2 Heat four tablespoons of olive oil in a pan over a high heat. Add the onion and fry for 3-4 minutes, then add the reserved tomato pulp and half of the basil leaves and season. Reduce the heat to medium, cover and continue to cook for 18-20 minutes, or until most of the moisture has evaporated and the mixture has thickened.

3 Heat two more tablespoons of olive oil in a separate pan. While the oil is heating up, sprinkle the flour onto a plate and dredge the aubergine rounds in the flour,

4 Dip each aubergine round into the beaten egg and add to the hot oil, in batches if necessary. Fry for 3-4 mins on each side, or until crisp and golden brown. Set aside to drain on kitchen paper. Add one fried aubergine slice to the cavity of each hollowed-out tomato, then layer with a spoonful of the tomato sauce, a basil leaf and a slice of mozzarella.

5 Repeat until the tomatoes are filled. Replace the 'lid' of each tomato and transfer to an ovenproof dish. Season and drizzle with olive oil. Bake the tomatoes in the oven for 20-25 minutes, until softened.

6 Garnish with any remaining basil leaves and a drizzle of olive oil. Season and serve.

SPICED CHICKEN BOWL

Ingredients

- 1 tbsp rapeseed oil
- 2 skinless chicken breasts
- 1 medium onion, sliced into 12 wedges
- 1 red pepper, deseeded and sliced
- 2 garlic cloves, finely chopped
- 100g/3½oz uncooked quinoa

- 100g/3½oz green beans, trimmed and cut in half
- ¼-½ tsp chilli flakes, according to taste
- 2 tsp ground cumin
- 2 tsp ground coriander
- 75g/3oz kale, thickly shredded

Method

1 Heat the oil in a large, deep frying pan or sauté pan. Season the chicken and fry over a medium-high heat for 2-3 mins each side or until golden. Transfer to a plate. Add the onion and pepper to the pan and cook for 3 mins, stirring, until softened and lightly browned.

2 Tip in the garlic and beans, and stir-fry for 2 mins. Add the chilli and spices, then stir in the quinoa. Pour in 700ml just-boiled water with 1/2 tsp flaked sea salt and bring to the boil.

3 Return the chicken to the pan, reduce the heat to a simmer and cook for 12 mins, stirring regularly and turning the chicken occasionally. Add the kale and cook for a further 3 mins or until the quinoa and chicken are cooked through.

CHEF'S NOTE
Quinoa (pronounced kinwa) is a healthy grain which is high in protein, dietary fibre and B vitamins - as such it's ok for occasional eating. Try it in place of rice or potatoes.

PULLED PORK

Ingredients

- 1.35kg/3lbs boneless pork shoulder
- 2 tsp cumin
- 2 tsp garlic powder
- 2 tsp onion powder
- 2 tsp salt
- 2 tsp paprika
- 2 tbsp hot sauce

Method

1 Add the pork shoulder to a large slow cooker.

2 In a small bowl, stir together the cumin, garlic powder, onion powder, salt, and paprika. Rub the mixture into the pork, being sure to coat all sides.

3 Pour the hot sauce into the bottom of the slow cooker.

4 Cook on low for 8 hours or high for 4 hours. The pork is ready when it easily shreds with a fork.

5 Shred the pork and stir the meat into the juices in the bottom of the slow cooker.

CHEF'S NOTE
This delicious meat is melt in the mouth soft, but contains none of the sugar bbq pulled pork has. Serve fajita style in lettuce wraps with guacamole and salsa.

MOULES MARINIERE

Ingredients

- 1.75kg/4lb mussels
- 1 garlic clove, finely chopped
- 2 shallots, finely chopped
- 15g/½oz butter
- A bouquet garni of parsley, thyme and bay leaves
- 100ml/3½floz dry white wine
- 120ml/4floz double cream
- Handful of parsley leaves, coarsely chopped

Method

1 Wash the mussels cold, running water. Discard any open ones that won't close when lightly squeezed.

2 Pull out the tough, fibrous beards protruding from the tightly closed shells, then knock off any barnacles with a large knife. Give the mussels another quick rinse to remove any little pieces of shell.

3 Soften the garlic and shallots in the butter with the bouquet garni, in a large pan big enough to take all the mussels - it should only be half full.

4 Add the mussels and wine, turn up the heat, cover and steam them open in their own juices for 3-4 mins. Give the pan a good shake every now and then.

5 Remove the bouquet garni, add the cream and chopped parsley then remove from the heat.

6 Spoon into four large warmed bowls and serve.

CHEF'S NOTE
This French classic is a restaurant staple, but mussels are relatively inexpensive and quick and easy to cook - so why not try them at home?

MEATLOAF AND GRAVY

Ingredients

- 2 tbsp butter
- 1 white onion, finely chopped
- 700g/1lb9oz minced beef
- 120ml/4floz double cream
- 60g/2½oz grated cheddar
- 1 egg
- 1 tsp salt
- 1 tbsp dried oregano or dried basil
- ½ tsp ground black pepper
- 200g/7oz sliced bacon
- 300ml/10½floz double cream, for the gravy

Method

1 Preheat the oven to 200C/400F/ Gas 6.

2 Fry the onion until soft but not browned.

3 Mix the beef in a bowl with all of the other ingredients, except the bacon. Mix well, but avoid overworking it because this can make the end result too dense.

4 Form into a loaf and place in a baking dish. Wrap the loaf in bacon.

5 Bake in the middle of the oven for about 45 minutes. If the bacon begins to overcook before the meat is done, cover with tin foil and lower the heat a bit.

6 Save the juices that have accumulated in the baking dish, and use to make the gravy. Mix the juices and the 300ml of cream in a smaller sauce pan.

7 Bring to a boil and lower the heat and let simmer for 10–15 minutes until it has the right consistency. Season to taste.

CHEF'S NOTE
This American classic is perfect served with freshly boiled broccoli or cauliflower with butter, salt and pepper. Contains no grains to thicken or bind.

GRAIN FREE PIZZA

Ingredients

- For the base:
- 150g/5oz mozzarella cheese
- 100g/3½oz almond flour
- 2 tbsp cream cheese
- 1 tsp white wine vinegar
- 1 egg
- ½ tsp salt

- For the topping:
- 6 cherry tomatoes, halved
- 1 tbsp butter
- 125ml/4floz tomato pasatta
- ½ tsp dried oregano
- 125g/4oz mozzarella cheese, shredded
- 6 torn basil leaves

Method

1 Preheat the oven to 200C/400F/ Gas 6. To make the base, heat the mozzarella and cream cheese in a small, non-stick pan on medium heat or in a bowl in the microwave oven. Stir until they melt together. Add the other ingredients and mix well.

2 Moisten your hands with oil and flatten the dough on parchment paper, making a circle about 8 inches (20 cm) in diameter.

3 Remove top parchment sheet (if used). Prick the crust all over with a fork and bake in the oven for 10–12 mins, until golden brown. Remove from the oven.

4 Spread a thin layer of tomato sauce on the crust. Top the pizza with tomatoes and plenty of cheese. Bake for 10–15 minutes, or until the cheese has melted. Top with the basil leaves and serve.

CHEF'S NOTE
Pizza may seem a no-go if you're avoiding grains, but using alternatives like almond flour means that you can still enjoy your favourites.

GRAIN free
BRAIN food

desserts

FRUIT FONDUE

Ingredients

- 300g/11oz mixed fruits, such as strawberries, pineapple chunks, grapes, mango chunks, melon chunks
- 150g/5oz double cream
- 100g/3½oz dark chocolate

Method

1 Thread the fruits onto wooden skewers.

2 Melt the chocolate on a low heat in the microwave or over a pan of boiling water with the double cream.

3 Transfer the sauce to a small serving bowl.

4 Serve the kebabs on a platter with chocolate sauce for dipping.

CHEF'S NOTE
Although milk chocolate may be out of bounds, dark chocolate is low in sugar meaning that it's ok to indulge once in a while, especially if you team with low-sugar fruits.

FRUITY BLANCMANGE

Ingredients

- 4 sheets leaf gelatine
- 6 tbsp sugar-free lemon squash
- ½ lemon, zest only, finely grated
- 150g/5oz natural yoghurt
- 200g/7oz mixed fresh or frozen berries

Method

1 Put the gelatine sheets in a medium bowl and cover with cold water. Leave to soak for 5 minutes, or until they soften. Turn them a couple of times to make sure they don't stick together.

2 Pour the squash, lemon zest and 100ml/3½fl oz of water into a small saucepan and heat very gently until just warm. Remove from the heat.

3 Squeeze the gelatine sheets to remove excess water and then add to the pan, stirring until it melts in to the liquid.

4 Stir in 250ml/9fl oz water and the yoghurt until they are thoroughly combined.

5 Pour the jelly into four glass tumblers or dishes, cover with cling film and chill for 5-6 hours, or overnight, until set.

6 Serve the jellies topped with fresh berries.

CHEF'S NOTE
Using sugar free squash in limited amounts is a great way to inject fruity flavours with no refined sugar. Experiment with different juices to find your favourite, but use sparingly as it is processed.

LIME AND MANGO PARFAIT

······················ *Ingredients* ·····················

- · 2 sheets leaf gelatine
- · 1 large ripe mango
  (approximately 450g/1lb)

- · 1 lime, finely grated zest only
- · 150ml/5floz double cream

······················ *Method* ·····················

1 Half fill a bowl with cold water and add the gelatine sheets one at a time. Leave to soak for 5 minutes.

2 Cut the mango in half either side of the large flat stone. Using a large spoon, scoop out the flesh and put into a food processor. Add the lime zest and blend until as smooth as possible.

3 Put 5 tablespoons of water in a saucepan and heat gently until lukewarm. Lift the gelatine sheets out of the cold water and carefully drop into the warm water, then stir vigorously with a wooden spoon for a few seconds until the gelatine dissolves. Remove from the heat.

4 Whip the cream using an electric whisk in a large bowl until it stands in fairly stiff peaks. With the motor running on the food processor, pour the gelatine solution slowly onto the mango purée and pulse until completely combined.

5 Put 6 tablespoons of the mango purée in a small bowl. Add the remaining purée to the whipped cream and whisk together lightly until smooth.

6 Spoon half the mango cream into four glass tumblers and spoon half the mango purée on top. Spoon the rest of the mango cream on top then finish with the remaining purée. Cover the dishes with cling film and chill for at least 3 hours before serving.

ARABIAN NIGHTS

Ingredients

- 2 x 150g/5½oz pots natural yoghurt
- 3 oranges
- Good pinch ground cinnamon
- 2 star anise

- ¼ tsp vanilla extract
- 10g/¼oz unsalted pistachio nuts, roughly chopped (alternatively use toasted flaked almonds)

Method

1 Cut one of the oranges in half and squeeze all the juice – you should end up with 4-5 tbsp. Peel the remaining oranges and cut into thin slices.

2 Pour the juice into a small saucepan and stir in the cinnamon, star anise and vanilla extract.

3 Place over a medium heat and simmer for 1-2 minutes, stirring occasionally. Add the orange slices and warm through gently.

4 Place the warm spiced oranges and juice into 2 bowls and spoon the yoghurt and scatter the nuts on top.

CHEF'S NOTE
This dessert is a refreshing taste of the middle-east. It has no refined sugar but plenty of sweetness from the juicy, spiced oranges.

SERVES 2

BLUEBERRY PUDDINGS

Ingredients

- 200g/7oz ricotta
- Pinch ground cinnamon
- 200g/7oz blueberries

Method

1 Mix the ricotta with the cinnamon.

2 Gently stir in most of the blueberries.

3 Divide the mixture between two ramekins or small bowls.

4 Top with the remaining blueberries and keep in the fridge, covered, until ready to eat.

CHEF'S NOTE
You may be more likely to encounter ricotta as part of a savory meal, but much like mascarpone this creamy cheese works perfectly when combined with sweet and fruity flavours.

CHOCOLATE TRUFFLES

Ingredients

- 120ml/4floz double cream
- 150g/5oz 85% dark chocolate
- 2 tbsp grass fed butter
- 2 tbsp stevia
- ½ tsp pure vanilla extract
- ½ tsp cinnamon
- 1 pinch sea salt
- 2 tbsp raw cocoa powder

Method

1 Heat the cream on a low flame, but don't let it boil. Chop the chocolate bar into small pieces.

2 When the cream is simmering, add the chopped chocolate and stir until combined. Add the butter and stir until completely melted.

3 Turn the heat off and add the stevia, vanilla, cinnamon, and salt. Stir to combine.

4 Let the mixture refrigerate for about an hour. You may need to stir every once in a while to ensure the butter is well distributed; it has a tendency to separate.

5 Once it's cool and hardened, you can scoop some truffle batter up and roll it into a small ball, about an inch and a half in diameter.

6 Place each round ball onto a plate lined with wax or parchment paper and refrigerate for about 30 minutes.

7 Place cocoa powder in a deep bowl and add your truffles. Shake and roll the truffles gently in the cocoa powder to coat them evenly.

CHEF'S NOTE
Perfect for when chocolate cravings hit, these deeply intense truffles are great to make a batch of and keep in the fridge ready for an occasional treat.

CHOCOLATE MOUSSE

···················· Ingredients ····················

- 225g/8oz cream cheese
- 125g/4oz dark chocolate, melted & cooled
- 100g/3½oz stevia
- 120ml/4floz double cream

···················· Method ····················

1 Beat the cream cheese and stevia until combined.

2 Add in the melted chocolate and beat to combine.

3 Slowly add in the cream, while beating on medium speed. Increase the speed to high and beat for 1-2 minutes, until creamy and fluffy.

4 Divide into 8 glasses or bowls and serve.

CHEF'S NOTE
This mousse makes a great dinner party dessert and can be topped with a swirl of whipped cream and a few blueberries for a show stopping finale.

LEMON GRANITA

Ingredients

- 120ml/4fl oz lemon juice
- 1 tsp lemon zest
- 250ml/8½floz water

- Stevia to taste (start with 1 tbsp and increase if needed)

Method

1 Combine the lemon juice, zest, water, and stevia in a bowl. Stir together well. Taste and adjust the sweetness to your liking by adding more stevia.

2 Pour the mixture into a large baking dish. It shouldn't be more than one inch deep.

3 Place in the freezer. After one hour, remove and scrap with a fork to break up the ice.

4 Place back in the freezer and continuing scraping every 30-40 mins until everything has turned to ice flakes.

CHEF'S NOTE
Zesty, fresh and greater than the sum of its parts. This is the dessert to eat when summer hits and you're in search of something to refresh and revive.

ICE LOLLIES

Ingredients

- 225g/8oz frozen mango, diced
- 225g/8oz frozen strawberries
- 250ml/8½oz Greek yogurt
- 120ml/4oz double cream
- 1 tsp vanilla extract

Method

1 Let mango and strawberries thaw for 10–15 mins.

2 Put all of the ingredients in a blender and mix until smooth.

3 Serve immediately as soft serve ice cream.

4 Alternatively pour into ice lolly forms and freeze for 1-2 hours before serving.

CHEF'S NOTE
Loved by adults and children alike, these ice lollies are a wonderful after dinner treat, with no grains or refined sugar.

BAKED APPLES WITH VANILLA CREAM

Ingredients

For the cream sauce:
- 600ml/1pt double cream
- ½ tsp vanilla extract
- 2 tbsp butter
- 1 egg yolk

For the baked apples:
- 3 tbsp butter
- 3 apples, preferably a type that is firm and tart
- 1 tsp ground cinnamon

Method

1 Add the butter and vanilla to a saucepan with about ¼ of the cream. Bring the mixture to a gentle boil by placing the sauce pan over medium heat. Lower the heat and let simmer for at least 5 minutes until the sauce turns creamy. Stir frequently.

2 Remove from the heat and add the egg yolk while whisking vigorously. Place in the refrigerator. You can prepare the flavored cream up to 1 day before and refrigerate.

3 Whisk the remaining cream in a bowl until soft peaks form, and fold into the refrigerated sauce.

4 Place back in the refrigerator for another 30 mins

5 Wash the apples, core and slice thinly. Heat up the butter in a frying pan and brown the slices until golden. Add the cinnamon towards the end.

6 Serve the apples warm with the vanilla sauce.

CHEF'S NOTE
Apple pie and custard is a winter staple but pastry is full of wheat and gluten which are bad for our health. This recipe gives you all of the taste but none of the drawbacks.

CHOCOLATE AND HAZELNUT SPREAD

Ingredients

- 150g/5oz hazelnuts
- 60ml/2floz coconut oil
- 30g/1oz unsalted butter
- 2 tbsp cocoa powder
- 1 tsp vanilla extract

Method

1 Roast the hazelnuts in a dry, hot frying pan until they turn a nice golden colour. Pay very close attention as the nuts will burn easily. Let them cool a little.

2 Place the nuts in a clean kitchen towel and rub so that some of the shells come off. The shells which are still stuck can stay there.

3 Place the nuts with all the remaining ingredients in a blender or a food processor. Blend to desired consistency. The longer you mix, the smoother the spread.

CHEF'S NOTE
Chocolate hazelnut spread is one of life's great joys. Eaten from the spoon is delicious, but serve with banana waffles for a dessert that's out of this world.

CHOCOLATE PEANUT BUTTER 'BROWNIES'

Ingredients

- 100g/3½oz dark chocolate with a minimum of 70% cocoa solids
- 4 tbsp butter or coconut oil
- 1 pinch salt
- 60ml/2floz peanut butter
- ½ tsp vanilla extract
- 60g/2oz chopped salted peanuts, for decoration

Method

1 Melt chocolate and butter or coconut oil in the microwave oven or in a double boiler.

2 Set the melted chocolate aside to cool for a few minute before proceeding with the next step.

3 Add all remaining ingredients, except the nuts, and blend until well combined.

4 Pour the batter into a small greased baking dish lined with parchment paper (no bigger than 4 x 6 inches).

5 Top with the finely chopped peanuts. Place in the refrigerator to chill.

CHEF'S NOTE

Rich and intense, you only need a small amount of this to be satisfied. Experiment with your own nut butters and grain free toppings.

COCONUT PUDDING

Ingredients

- 400g/14oz coconut milk
- 2 tbsp coconut sugar
- 2 eggs
- 2 tbsp + 1 tsp arrowroot powder
- 1 tsp pure vanilla extract
- 2 tbsp butter, cut into small pieces

Method

1 Add the coconut milk and sugar to a small pan and heat over low-medium heat, bringing it to a simmer.

2 Meanwhile, whisk the eggs and add in the arrowroot powder.

3 Pour one ladle of the steaming milk into the egg mixture, whisking constantly to prevent clumping.

4 Turn the pot of coconut milk to low and slowly add the egg mixture, whisking until thickened.

5 Once it has thickened, remove from heat and stir in the vanilla and butter.

6 Pour into four small bowls, or mason jars, cover and cool until well chilled.

CHEF'S NOTE

A kind of coconut custard, this tropical delight goes well with a few raspberries or cherries. Try scattering a few chopped nuts on top for added texture.

MACAROONS

- 30g/1¼oz organic almond flour
- 60g/2½oz shredded coconut
- 2 tbsp stevia
- 1 tbsp vanilla extract

- 1 tbsp coconut oil
- 3 egg whites

Method

1 Preheat the oven to 200C/400F/Gas 6.

2 In a bowl, mix together the almond flour, coconut and stevia until well blended.

3 Melt the coconut oil in a small saucepan and add the vanilla extract.

4 In the meantime, chill a medium bowl in the freezer for mounting the egg whites.

5 Add the melted coconut oil to the flour mixture and blend really well.

6 Put the egg whites in the chilled bowl and whisk until stiff.

7 Gently incorporate the egg whites

into the flour mixture, trying to not over mix and to preserve some of the volume from the eggs whites.

8 Spoon the mixture into 10 piles on a baking sheet.

9 Bake for 8 mins, or until macaroons start to brown on top.

10 Remove from oven and allow cool.

CHEF'S NOTE

Not to be confused with the brightly coloured and crisp French macarons, these are damp and squidgy in the middle and perfect with an after dinner coffee.

STRAWBERRY CHEESECAKES

Ingredients

- 225g/8oz mascarpone cheese
- 250ml/8½floz double cream
- ¾ tsp vanilla stevia drops
- 225g/8oz strawberries

Method

1 Whip together the mascarpone, cream and stevia in large mixing bowl with electric mixer until well combined.

2 Pipe into individual cups and layer with the strawberries.

CHEF'S NOTE
These cheesecakes may have no biscuit base but they're so delicious, quick and easy to make that you won't even notice!

GRAIN free
BRAIN food

sides,
starters
& snacks

BLUE CHEESE DRESSING

Ingredients

- 150g/5oz blue cheese
- 175ml/7floz Greek yogurt
- 120ml/4floz mayonnaise
- 2 tbsp fresh parsley, finely chopped

Method

1 Place the cheese into a small bowl and use a fork to break it up into coarse chunks.

2 Add yoghurt and mayonnaise and mix well.

3 Let sit for a few minutes to allow the flavours to develop.

4 Add salt and pepper to taste before serving.

CHEF'S NOTE
Deeply savoury and creamy, this sauce works well as a salad dressing with chicken and bacon, a dip for celery or even as a condiment to leftover roast beef.

GRAIN FREE NAAN BREAD

Ingredients

- 50 g/2oz coconut flour
- 1 tbsp ground psyllium husk powder
- ¼ tsp onion powder

- ¼ tsp baking powder
- ½ tsp salt
- 2 tbsp melted coconut oil
- 225ml/8floz boiling water

Method

1 Mix all the dry ingredients in a bowl. Add the oil and boiling water (hold some of it back in case it's not needed) and stir thoroughly.

2 Allow to rise for 5 minutes. The dough will turn firm fairly quickly, but stay flexible. It should resemble the consistency of Play-Doh. If you find it's too runny, then add more psyllium husk until it feels right. If it's too firm, add some of the remaining water. The amount needed may vary depending on what brand of husk or coconut flour you use.

3 Divide into 4 pieces and form into balls, then flatten with your hands directly on parchment paper or on the kitchen counter.

4 Fry the rounds in a skillet over medium heat until the Naan turns a nice golden colour.

5 Keep the bread warm in a low oven until you're ready to serve.

CHEF'S NOTE
Naan bread is usually full of refined grains, hidden sugars and is terrible for your brain health. This version goes particularly well with the vegetable curry. Alternatively top with cheese and tomatoes for a cheat's pizza.

MARINATED OLIVES

Ingredients

- 1½ tbsp coriander seeds
- 1 lemon
- 200g/7oz Kalamata olives
- 200g/7oz green queen olives
- Extra virgin olive oil

Method

1 Use a pestle and mortar to coarsely crush the coriander seeds.

2 Peel off long thick strips of lemon zest and place in a bowl with the olives.

3 Squeeze the lemon juice over and then top with 3 times as much extra virgin olive oil.

4 Add salt, pepper and the crushed coriander seeds. Pour the dressing over the olives and leave to marinate.

CHEF'S NOTE
These olives can be made well in advance for a healthy snack. The longer you leave them, the better they'll taste.

VEGETABLE CRISPS

·················· *Ingredients* ··················

- 125g/4oz swede
- 125g/4oz carrot
- 100g/3½oz parsnip
- 100g/3½oz beetroot
- Spray oil

······················ *Method* ······················

1 Preheat the oven to 180C/35F/ Gas 4. Slice the vegetables very thinly.

2 Spray a little oil over a baking sheet and arrange the vegetable slices, ensuring they don't overlap.

3 Cook for 20 minutes, until lightly browned. Turn the vegetables frequently, as they can easily burn. You may need to remove some crisps before the 20 minutes is up, as some will cook faster than others.

4 When all the crisps are ready, allow them to cool then mix together and serve.

CHEF'S NOTE
Crisps are best avoided in order to ensure good brain health, but if cravings strike, make this healthier version with mixed vegetables and no potatoes.

CHICKEN LIVER PATE

Ingredients

- 1 tbsp olive oil
- 2 shallots, finely chopped
- 3 sprigs thyme, leaves only
- 1 garlic clove, crushed
- A pinch freshly grated nutmeg
- ½ tsp ground allspice
- Zest of 1 orange

- 400g/14oz chicken livers, trimmed of any membrane and gristle, roughly chopped
- 50ml/2floz brandy
- 100ml/3½floz double cream
- 120g/4½oz unsalted butter, cubed

Method

1 Heat the oil in a frying pan over a medium heat. Add the shallots and thyme and cook gently for 5 mins, or until soft. Add the garlic, spices, orange zest and a good pinch of salt and pepper and cook for a further 2 mins.

2 Add the chicken livers to the pan and fry for 6-8 mins, or until just cooked through. Remove from the heat and spoon everything into a food processor. Blend until smooth.

3 Add the brandy to the pan to deglaze, then add the cream and bring to a simmer. Cook for 2 minutes, stirring throughout.

4 Pour into the food processor and blend until smooth. With the motor running, gradually add the cubed butter and blend until smooth.

5 Pass the mixture through a fine sieve into a bowl, then divide between four ramekins. Smooth the tops down by banging the bottom of the ramekins against the work surface, then place in the fridge to set.

CHEF'S NOTE
This pate makes a great starter if you have guests or even just an indulgent lunch or snack. Try serving with the grain free crispbreads and some cornichons.

CREAM CHEESE CRUDITÉS

Ingredients

- 50g/2oz cream cheese
- ½ tsp olive oil
- 1 tbsp chopped fresh parsley or fresh basil
- 1 garlic clove
- Zest of ½ lemon
- 1 celery stalk, or other fresh vegetables of your liking

Method

1 Stir all of the ingredients into the cream cheese.

2 Let sit in the refrigerator for at least 10 mins to let all of the flavours develop. Add salt if needed.

3 Rinse the celery stalk, cut into 2-3 inch lengths, and serve together with the soft cheese.

CHEF'S NOTE

This cheese is delicious as a savoury snack with crudités, but consider making extra to stuff into chicken breasts before roasting, or to spread over ham slices before rolling up and eating.

SMOKED SALMON FILLED AVOCADO

Ingredients

- 2 avocados
- 175ml/6floz crème fraîche, sour cream or mayonnaise
- 2 tbsp lemon juice (optional)
- 175g/6oz smoked salmon

Method

1 Cut the avocados in half and remove the pit.

2 Place a dollop of crème fraiche, sour cream or mayonnaise in the hollow of the avocado.

3 Add the smoked salmon on top.

4 Season to taste with salt, pepper and a squeeze lemon juice before serving.

CHEF'S NOTE
Full of healthy fats, this works as a great starter for a dinner party, or even a healthy breakfast. It also works well with other fatty fish such as smoked mackerel or trout.

SESAME SEED CRISPBREADS

Ingredients

- 175g/6oz sesame seeds
- 60g/2½oz sunflower seeds
- 60g/2½oz grated hard cheese
- 1 tbsp ground psyllium husk powder
- 100ml/3½floz water
- 2 eggs
- ¼ - 1 tsp salt

Method

1 Preheat the oven to 180C/350F/ Gas 5

2 Mix together all of the ingredients and spread out on parchment paper on a baking sheet. Sprinkle sea salt on top and then bake for 20 mins.

3 Remove and carefully cut the crackers into the desired form

4 Lower the heat to 140C/ 275F/ Gas 1 and cook for another 40 minutes.

5 Remove the crispbreads and make sure they're dry all of the way through.

CHEF'S NOTE
These crispbreads make a great accompaniment to dips or cheese and are perfect for an after-dinner snack.

GUACAMOLE

Ingredients

- 2 ripe avocados
- 1 garlic clove
- Juice of ½ lime
- 3tbsp olive oil

- ½ white onion
- Small bunch of fresh coriander
- 1 diced tomato

Method

1 Peel the avocados and mash with a fork. Grate or chop the onion finely and add to the avocado.

2 Squeeze the lime and add the juice to the avocado mix.

3 Add the tomato, olive oil and finely chopped coriander. Season with salt and pepper and mix well.

CHEF'S NOTE
Guacamole is a Mexican staple. Try as a dip with the sesame seed crispbreads, or atop pulled pork in lettuce wraps.

DEVILLED EGGS

Ingredients

- 6 eggs
- 1 heaped tbsp mayonnaise
- ½ tsp salt
- ½ tsp pepper
- 1 heaped tsp mustard
- 1 tbsp paprika powder to garnish

Method

1 Boil the eggs by placing in cold water, bring the water to a boil and cook for 10mins.

2 Place the eggs in cold water and let them chill for 5 mins.

3 Peel the eggs and slice lengthwise. Scoop yolks out and place in a separate bowl. Place the eggs whites on extra plate.

4 Add all the other ingredients (except paprika powder) to the yolks and mix until creamy.

5 Spoon the mixture into the egg whites and sprinkle with the paprika powder.

CHEF'S NOTE

Eggs are a superfood on a no grain diet and are packed with protein. The mayonnaise adds healthy fats and the spices make this a bit more special.

CHEESE LOLLYPOPS

Ingredients

- 80g/3oz Parmesan, finely grated
- 1 tsp poppy seeds
- 1 tsp sesame seeds
- Butter, for greasing
- 10 lollypop sticks

Method

1 Preheat the oven to 220C/425F/Gas 7. Line two large baking trays with baking paper and grease them with butter.

2 Mix the cheese and seeds together in a small bowl. Sit a 9cm/3½in chefs' ring or cookie cutter on one of the baking trays and sprinkle a small handful of the cheese mixture into it, in a thin layer. Carefully lift the ring off to reveal a neat-edged disc of Parmesan and lay a lollipop stick on top, with the tip of the stick touching the middle of the disc.

3 Repeat with the remaining cheese and sticks to make 10 in total (leaving about 3cm/1¼in spaces between them to allow for any spreading during cooking).

4 You should have a little Parmesan left over, so use it to cover up the part of the lollipop stick resting on the disc.

5 Bake in the oven for 5 minutes, swapping the lollipops to a different shelf halfway through. The cheese should be lightly golden-brown and bubbling.

6 Remove from the oven and slide the paper off the baking trays and onto a rack to help speed up cooling. Leave to cool for 1–2 mins, or until the lollipops have become crisp. Very carefully remove each one with a palette knife.

BAKED CHEESE

Ingredients

- 200g/7oz Brie or Camembert wheel
- 1 tbsp olive oil
- Fresh rosemary leaves

Method

1 Preheat the oven to 170C/350F/Gas 4

2 Drizzle the cheese with olive oil and top with rosemary.

3 Bake until soft and starting to ooze (this should take around 10 mins.)

4 Serve immediately.

CHEF'S NOTE
A baked cheese is an indulgent dinner party or special occasion starter. Serve with crispbreads, carrot sticks, gherkins or sliced apple.

CURRIED CAULIFLOWER

Ingredients

- 1 large head of cauliflower, broken into florets
- 2 garlic cloves, crushed
- 2 tsp each caraway and cumin seed
- 3 tbsp olive oil
- 100g/3½oz pine nuts
- Small bunch each parsley and dill, leaves torn

Method

1 Heat oven to 200C/180C fan/Gas 6.

2 Toss the cauliflower, garlic, spices, 2 tbsp oil and some seasoning in a roasting tin.

3 Roast the cauliflower for 30 mins.

4 Add the pine nuts and remaining oil to the tin, then cook for 10 mins more.

5 To serve, stir in the herbs.

CHEF'S NOTE

Cauliflower is perhaps one of the most adaptable vegetables for you to eat if you're limiting your grain consumption. This curried version goes well with meat or fish.

FETA STUFFED PEPPERS

Ingredients

- 4 red peppers
- 1 courgette, quartered lengthways and thinly sliced
- 2 x 250g/9oz packs ready-to-eat quinoa

- 85g/3¼oz feta cheese, finely crumbled
- Handful parsley, roughly chopped

Method

1 Heat oven to 200C/180C fan/Gas 6. Cut each pepper in half through the stem, and remove the seeds. Put the peppers, cut-side up, on a baking sheet, drizzle with 1 tbsp olive oil and season well. Roast for 15 mins.

2 Meanwhile, heat 1 tbsp olive oil in a small frying pan, add the courgette and cook until soft. Remove from the heat, then stir through the quinoa, feta and parsley. Season with pepper.

3 Divide the quinoa mixture between the pepper halves, then return to the oven for 5 mins to heat through.

CHEF'S NOTE
These stuffed peppers make a great side dish, or can be served as the star of the show, with a dressed salad on the side.

SPICED NUTS

Ingredients

- 1 egg white
- 2 tsp Chinese five-spice powder
- ½ tsp salt

- 85g/3¼oz each pecans and almonds

Method

1 Heat oven to 150C/324F fan/Gas 2.

2 Lightly whisk egg white, then add Chinese five spice and salt.

3 Add the sunflower and pumpkin seeds, and coat well.

4 Spread out in a single layer on a lightly oiled baking sheet and bake for 12 mins. Cool before eating.

CHEF'S NOTE
Nuts are a great source of protein and healthy fats, making them a perfect snack. This version has a slight kick, making them a great dish for when you're entertaining.